ASSISI

where to find

THE PRIMITIVE PAINTERS
CIMABUE
GIOTTO
SIMONE MARTINI
PIETRO LORENZETTI

Giovanna Mariucci

SCALA

2

5

Sacro
Convento

3

4

piazza
inferiore di
San Francesco

piazza
superiore di
San Francesco

porta
San Francesco

Largo
San Pietro

via Marconi

via San Francesco

San Pietro

via del Fosso Cupo

Portico di
Monte
Frumentario

Osservatorio
Cristiano

ta di
nentone

via Sant'Apollinare

via Cristofani

Rocca
Maggiore

Palazzo del
Capitano del
Popolo

Palazzo
dei Priori

porta
Moiano

via Sant'Agnese

Corso Mazzini

Palazzo
dei Consoli

1

piazza
Santa
Chiara

Duomo

Teatro
Romano

porta
Perlici

Fonte
Santureggio

piazza
Matteotti

Anfiteatro
Romano

viale Vittorio Emanuele II

via Borgo Aretino

Rocca
Minore

porta
Nuova

porta

© 2004 SCALA Group S.p.A., Florence
All rights reserved

The illustrations in this volume have been supplied
by the SCALA PICTURE LIBRARY,
the largest source of color transparencies and digital
images of the visual arts in the world.

The over 60,000 subjects visible at the site
www.scalarchives.it
can be accessed through computerized procedures
that permit easy and rapid picture searches of any
complexity.

e-mail: archivio@scalagroup.com

Photographs: SCALA PICTURE LIBRARY

The images from the SCALA PICTURE LIBRARY
reproducing cultural assets that belong to the Italian
State are published with the permission of the
Ministry for Cultural Heritage and Activities.

Translation: Huw Evans
Printed by: "Arti Grafiche" Stampa Nazionale
Calenzano (Florence), 2004

THE BASILICAS OF ASSISI

SAN FRANCESCO

Work on the basilica commenced in 1228, two years after Francis's death, on the orders of Pope Gregory IX, and was carried out under the supervision of Brother Elias, one of the saint's early companions. In 1253 the church was consecrated and St. Francis's body brought there for reburial. The work must have been completed by 1280.

The basilica is made up of two churches, one set on top of the other, with a T-shaped plan echoing the shape of the cross: the Lower Church, used for the religious services of the friars and cloaked in semidarkness, with lower ceilings and massive piers; and the Upper Church, tall, graceful and filled with light, intended for solemn celebrations and as a place of pilgrimage. Thus the building represents a remarkable passage from the traditional forms of the Umbrian Romanesque-Gothic to a free interpretation of Northern European Gothic. The construction was followed by a long and uninterrupted activi-

Plan of the Upper Church

Left, the nave of the Upper Church looking toward the altar

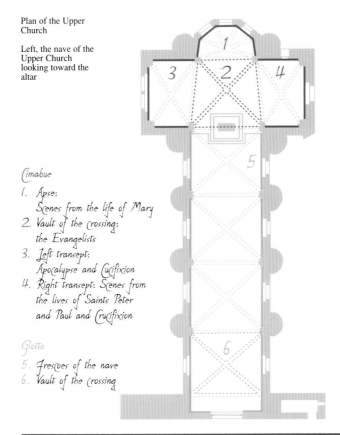

Cimabue
1. Apse:
    Scenes from the life of Mary
2. Vault of the crossing:
    the Evangelists
3. Left transept:
    Apocalypse and Crucifixion
4. Right transept: Scenes from
    the lives of Saints Peter
    and Paul and Crucifixion

Giotto
5. Frescoes of the nave
6. Vault of the crossing

View of the nave of the Upper Church looking toward the altar

out was that of the stained-glass windows, among the oldest and most important in Italy, for which craftsmen were brought in from Germany and France.

The pictorial decoration, on which work started in the second half of the 13th century, allows us to trace the evolution and renewal of Italian art in the Duecento and Trecento through the work of all the most important painters of the time. Thus San Francesco became the crucible of the principal innovations in European painting, in terms of technique as well as iconography and composition, thanks to the fact that artists of the highest skill and different backgrounds came together to collaborate on this great undertaking of an international character. In fact the Franciscan basilica was the most important church in Christendom of its day, just as it was the center of the greatest religious movement to have emerged in the West after the advent of Christianity.

ty of decoration, carried out by artists and craftsmen of diverse formation and geographical origin. Fierce critical debate has arisen over the dates and authorship of the interventions, and has not yet come to a conclusion: what is certain is that the first part of the decoration to be carried

After the tragic earthquake of 1997, which brought down some of the frescoes, the basilica is now open to visitors again, thanks to careful and demanding restorations.

Plan of the Lower Church

Facing page, transept and portal of the Lower Church

Cimabue

1. Fresco of the vault: Madonna and Child Enthroned, with four Angels and Saint Francis

Giotto

2. Vault and rear wall
3. Vaulting cells of the presbytery
4. Chapel of the Maddalena
5. Chapel of San Nicola

Pietro Lorenzetti

6. Walls of the transept

Simone Martini

7. Chapel of San Martino
8. Lower fresco: five Saints

SANTA CHIARA

L ocated at the opposite end of the city of Assisi to the basilica dedicated to Francis, the basilica of Santa Chiara was intended to represent the complementary pole of Franciscan spirituality, the female one. Work on it started in 1257 and in 1260 the body of St. Clare was translated there. The building presents similarities to the Upper Church of San Francesco: it too has a Latin-cross plan, with a projecting transept. But it also reflects a greater desire for simplicity, in keeping with the aspirations of the Minorite Order, also known as the Poor Clares, which in 1253 had wrested the privilege of poverty from the pontiff. As in San Francesco, the rich fresco decoration of the walls, illustrating Clare's life in a clear parallel with Giotto's frescoes devoted to the founder, was supposed to contrast with the simplicity of the architecture, but the cycle was almost totally lost between the 18th and 19th century. On the left-hand side of the nave is set the chapel of San Giorgio, which used to be part of the original small church where the remains of both saints had been taken to await the completion of their respective basilicas. It now contains the celebrated *Crucifix of San Damiano*.

The church also houses two panels by the so-called Master of St. Clare, the *Madonna and Child* in the left transept and *Saint Clare and Scenes from Her Life* in the right transept.

The basilica of Santa Chiara was also badly damaged in the 1997 earthquake, which seriously compromised its structure. After a long and difficult intervention of restoration, the church has been completely reopened to the public.

Top, view of Santa Chiara; bottom, the campanile

SANTA MARIA DEGLI ANGELI

The name "Portiuncola" had been used, since the 11th century, for a flat area of land at the foot of Assisi, covered by a dense wood. Here stood a small chapel dedicated to the Virgin of which Francis was particularly fond: he often came there in search of silence and chose it as the place to die. The area became an important center of the Franciscan cult, especially after the indulgence of the Feast of the Pardon granted in 1277, which offered the remission of sins to all the faithful who visited the chapel between vespers on August 1 and vespers on August 2. At the conclusion of the Council of Trent, Pius V decided to construct a large basilica on the site: it was erected between 1569 and 1679, to a design drawn up by Galeazzo Alessi and approved by Vignola. It is a huge building with a nave and two aisles, much of it rebuilt following the earthquakes of the 19th century.

Inside it, beneath the dome, stands the "Portiuncola" or "Porziuncola," the tiny Romanesque church of Santa Maria degli Angeli, dating from the 10th-11th century, where Francis founded the order of the Friars Minor and where, in 1212, he gave the veil to Clare. On the outside it is decorated with paintings by Friedrich Overbeck (1829) and Perugino (1486); inside there is a large panel by Ilario da Viterbo (1393).

At the beginning of the presbytery, on the right, stands the chapel of the Transi-

Top, the grotto of St. Francis; alongside, the "Porziuncola" inside the basilica

The chapel of the Transito and the chapel
of the Roseto

to, the cell where Francis died on October 3, 1226, which still has its original walls and wooden door. In a niche above the altar is set a glazed terracotta statue of *Saint Francis* by Andrea della Robbia. From the sacristy you can take a tour of various rooms connected with Francis's life and the legends that have grown up around him: the Roseto, a tiny garden in which roses grow without thorns, and the chapel of the Roseto, with the oratory of San Bonaventura and the grotto underneath, constructed in the place where Francis used to dwell. Finally the small chapel of the Pianto, dedicated to meditation on Christ's Passion.

At the end of the tour you come to what remains of the "conventino" or little monastery, built by Bernardine of Siena in the 15th century. It now houses the Museo della Basilica, where you can see, among other works, Giunta Pisano's *Crucifix* and the panel representing *Saint Francis* by the Master of St. Francis.

FRANCISCAN ICONOGRAPHY

St. Francis's physical appearance was described by Tommaso da Celano, his first biographer, who knew him and portrayed him as a slim, dark-haired man with a penetrating gaze. Very often, however, it is the tendency to idealize and normalize Francis's figure that prevails in his representation. While in the panel in Santa Maria degli Angeli there is a vague hint of the slenderness of the saint's body, in the cycle of paintings in the Lower Church by the Master of St. Francis we find the first official and monumental definition of the image of the order's founder.

In this context the portrait by Cimabue, again in the Lower Church, has an almost revolutionary value, in its recovery of the tangibility of the historical personage. Giotto, in the Upper Church, proves even more classicist than St. Bonaventure, who was responsible for a "purge" of the image of Franciscanism most strictly linked to poverty: in the *Dream of Innocent III* Francis is presented as a champion, in the grandiloquent pose of an ancient statue.

The absence of the beard, an attribute that we know to have been characteristic of the real Francis, was a polemical stance taken against the current of the Spirituals. In fact the only 14th-century images of Francis with a beard in Assisi are the ones by Simone Martini, commissioned by the Angevins, who were great supporters of the Spirituals.

Anonymous Pisan painter
(Master of the Treasury),
*Saint Francis and Four of His
Miracles*, detail, Museo del
Tesoro della Basilica, Assisi

Master of St. Francis,
Saint Francis, detail,
Santa Maria degli Angeli, Assisi

Master of St. Francis,
*Saint Francis Preaching
to the Birds*, detail,
San Francesco, Assisi

Cimabue, *Madonna and Child
with Angels and Saint Francis*,
detail, San Francesco, Assisi

Giotto, *The Dream of Innocent III*,
detail, San Francesco, Assisi

Simone Martini, *Saint Francis*,
San Francesco, Assisi

THE "PRIMITIVE" PAINTERS

Already during Francis's lifetime, and to an even greater extent after his death and speedy canonization, the Franciscan Order and the cult of its founder spread at an extraordinary rate. This enthusiasm found expression, from the artistic viewpoint, in the production of panel paintings of a devotional character: mostly these were images of Francis, Clare (who was regarded as his female counterpart), and Christ Crucified, to which the saint had been especially devoted. It was only later, with the foundation of the two basilicas and their decoration around the middle of the 13th century, that imposing cycles of frescoes were conceived and realized. At that point the work of the 13th-century artists and craftsmen was continued, without a break, by the Tuscans and Romans who took turns working on the great basilica of San Francesco throughout the following century.

The majority of the authors of the 13th-century masterpieces remain anonymous and are identified by names that refer to their most important works. Some of the attributions to their catalogue are still controversial, but what emerges clearly is the extreme vivacity and variety of the artistic milieu that grew up around the Franciscan Order in Assisi. Here different artistic influences came together and gave rise to a new figurative language. From Giunta Pisano (*floruit* 1229-54), the great renewer of the iconography of the Byzantine tradition of the crucifix, to the Master of St. Francis (second half of the 13th century), perhaps the greatest Umbrian painter of the time, Jacopo Torriti (second half of the 13th century), a refined Roman painter in close contact with Pietro Cavallini, and the Master of the Arrest of Christ (late 13th century), a probable collaborator with Giotto's workshop, it is possible to trace a coherent course of development that is rich in outstanding personalities and diverse stylistic solutions and choices.

Enormous resources were channeled into the celebration of the Franciscan Order and its founder, in financial as well as organizational terms, and very often contributions were made by the popes themselves. Their munificent gifts formed the core of the basilica's Treasury, which, despite being plundered several times over the centuries, still boasts a rich collection. Among the more valuable objects, it is worth singling out the *Chalice of Nicholas IV*, a masterpiece by the Sienese Guccio di Mannaia (documented in Siena from 1291 to 1318).

The unknown author of the *Crucifix of San Damiano* deserves separate discussion. Active in an earlier period than the one under examination, he is mentioned here for the historical and artistic value of the work and for the importance that this assumed from the devotional viewpoint right from the earliest days of Franciscanism.

Left, Master of
Saint Francis,
*The Preaching
to the Birds*,
Lower Church, Assisi

BASILICA OF SANTA CHIARA

Crucifix of San Damiano, late 12th century

The crucifix comes from the church of San Damiano, where in 1205, according to tradition, it spoke to Francis, asking him to repair the church. It is a typical example of the painted crosses that became widespread from the middle of the 12th century in the territory of Pisa and Lucca. On a support made of wood, or parchment applied to wood, they represented Christ on the cross surrounded by scenes of the Passion. These crucifixes were hung on the triumphal arch or set above the iconostasis, as can clearly be seen in some of Giotto's frescoes in the Upper Church of San Francesco (*The Verification of the Stigmata*, *The Crib at Greccio*) and above all in the scene that faithfully depicts this very cross, inside the dilapidated church of San Damiano. The oldest dated example is the one in Sarzana Cathedral, signed by Master Guglielmo in 1138: like this one, it represents Christ frontally, still alive, in accordance with the iconography of Christ *triumphans*. In the 13th century the scheme of the dead and suffering Christ, with his body arched and head slumped, began to spread out from the area of Pisa: the typology is that of Christ *patiens*, of Byzantine origin.

Giotto, *The Admonition of the Crucifix of San Damiano*, Upper Church, San Francesco, Assisi

Master of Santa Chiara, *Saint Clare and Scenes from Her Life*, 1283

Giunta Pisano exercised an influence on some of the best painters in the region between Assisi and Perugia in the second half of the 13th century, as in the case of the Master of Santa Chiara, who takes his name from this altarpiece, now in the left transept of the basilica dedicated to the saint. The same church houses a *Crucifix* by the same artist, executed sometime before 1260 for the abbess Benedetta, and another panel with the *Madonna Enthroned*, dated 1265 and mentioned in a document that names its author: Benvenuto Benvieni da Foligno. This was an artist who, commencing his activity under the influence of Giunta and in a style that still displayed vestiges of the Romanesque, went on to develop, through his encounter with the cultivated and elegant expressionism of the Master of St. Francis, solutions of a marked lyricism that make him a typical exponent of late 13th-century Umbrian painting.

BASILICA OF SANTA MARIA DEGLI ANGELI

Giunta Pisano, *Crucifix*, before 1236

Franciscan patronage was responsible for a remarkable surge in the production of painted crucifixes, in memory of the one in the church of San Damiano that, according to tradition, had spoken to St. Francis. In 1236 Brother Elias, the first general of the order, commissioned a cross for the Upper Church of San Francesco in Assisi from Giunta. However, that cross should not be identified with the one in Santa Maria degli Angeli, which may be older.

The reference to the Byzantine formula of the suffering Christ in Giunta's work is enriched with a powerful dramatic tension and a genuine sense of emotional involvement. The more archaic scheme of the crucifix-altarpiece, with scenes at the sides, like that of San Damiano, is replaced by a simpler one, which enhances the drama by isolating Christ's figure. The tension of the arched body, with the slumped head, is underlined to suggest the prolongation of Jesus's agony and pain even after death.

MUSEO DELLA BASILICA DI SANTA MARIA DEGLI ANGELI

Master of St. Francis, *Saint Francis among Angels,* *c.* 1250

The wooden panel on which the picture is painted was used as a pallet by the saint in life and in death, as the inscription tells us: "*hic lectus mihi fuit et viventi et morienti.*" It is possible to discern an attempt at characterization of the figure of the saint, despite the fixity of the icon, with its rigorously frontal representation. The figures of the angels are reminiscent, in the elegance of their line and color, of the products of the most refined Byzantine tradition.

TREASURY, BASILICA OF SAN FRANCESCO

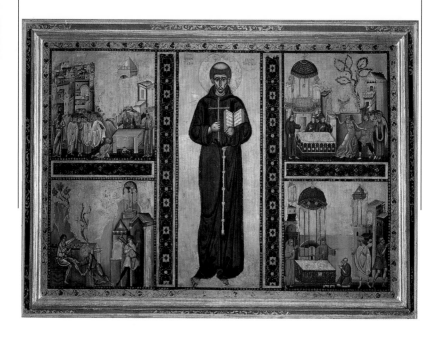

Master of the Treasury, *Saint Francis and Four of His Miracles*, between 1250 and 1260

The picture, now in the Museo del Tesoro, was originally located in the Orsini Chapel, in the Lower Church, and was painted on a wooden panel that was used to wash the saint's body after his death. So it is a sort of relic, on which four miracles worked by Francis are depicted: *The Miracle of the Little Girl with Her Head Stuck to Her Shoulder*, *The Healing of Bartolomeo da Narni*, *The Casting Out of a Devil from a Girl* and *The Miracle of a Cripple*.

The author has been variously identified as Giunta Pisano, Bonaventura Berlinghieri and others. In all likelihood, however, he was a local painter who, in the lively circles of Franciscan figurative culture, came under the influence of different artistic currents, ranging from the painting of the region of Pisa and Lucca to that of Byzantium and Palestine, as well as the Venetian miniature.

Bonaventura
Berlinghieri,
*Saint Francis and
Scenes from His Life*,
Santa Croce, Florence

"Historiated panels"
representing episodes
from the life of St.
Francis were produced
in large numbers in
the 13th century, but
their production went
into decline as the
grand mural cycles
grew more common.

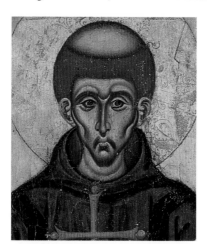

Master of the Blue Crucifixes, *Crucifix*,
second half of the 13th century

The cross in the Museo del Tesoro is painted on both sides
and was probably originally hung underneath the vault of
the high altar of the Lower Church. The anonymous author is an
Umbrian painter, very active after the middle of the 13th century, whose work shows the great influence exercised on this generation of artists by the pictures painted in Assisi by Giunta
Pisano and by the activity, fundamental for the pictorial culture
of these regions, of the Master of St. Francis. This artist too received a training in the Byzantine manner that was enlivened by
the influence of the emerging Gothic culture. He is considered
one of the most refined painters of the 13th century in Umbria.

The chalice was commissioned especially for the basilica by Nicholas IV, the first Franciscan pope, who reigned from 1288 to 1292. The gift was linked to an indulgence of forty days.

Guccio di Mannaia, *Chalice of Pope Nicholas IV*, *c.* 1290

This marvelous work, which has been in the rich Treasury of the basilica since the outset, is the only one that can be attributed to the Sienese artist with certainty.

It is made of silver, cast by the lost-wax process, chased, engraved and gilded. Its exceptional character in the history of the Sienese goldwork is due to the use, for the first time, of the technique of translucent enamel. This allows delicate shadings of color to be produced by laying successive coats of transparent enamel over the very low relief of the embossing. These enamels, notwithstanding the precocity of their appearance, display a great mastery of the technique and style and show that the author was familiar with examples of French gold work and contemporary Sienese painting. The chalice is decorated with ninety-six medallions, in twelve rows of eight, that follow a complex iconographic program in which the miracle of the Eucharist is linked to the redeeming role of the Crucifixion, in the version of humility given to it by Franciscan mysticism.

In the oldest inventory of the basilica, compiled in 1298, the work is described as a *"calix argenteus et inauratus pretiosus."*

Jacopo Torriti, *Face of God the Creator*, sinopia, 1288-92

The drawing, traced in reddish-brown chalk on the plaster, was found in the nave of the Upper Church of Assisi underneath the fresco depicting the *Creation*. The refined handling of the head of God the Creator, accurately represented in its outlines and shading, demonstrates the great skill of the artist who drew it, the Roman Jacopo Torriti.

UPPER CHURCH, SAN FRANCESCO

Creation of the World
Creation of Eve

Jacopo Torriti, *Vault of the Deesis;*
Scenes of Creation, Annunciation, Marriage
at Cana, 1288-92

B efore his prestigious intervention in San Giovanni in Laterano, Jacopo Torriti had probably worked in Assisi at the
head of a team of Roman painters that had been entrusted with
the decoration of the Upper Church of San Francesco, left un-
finished after Cimabue's work in the presbytery. Torriti seems
to have been responsible for the frescoes on the ceiling of the
second bay, called the vault of the Deesis, in which the figures
of the Virgin, the Redeemer, St. John the Baptist and St. Francis are represented. Other scenes on the walls beneath are attributed to him, including the *Creation of the World*, the *Creation of Eve*, the *Construction of Noah's Ark*, the *Annunciation*
and the *Marriage at Cana*.

Facing page:
Construction of Noah's
Ark and *Marriage*
at Cana
On pages 26-7: *vault of*
the Deesis

Master of the Arrest of Christ, *Nativity*, *c*. 1280-90

This artist, of local origin, was active in the Upper Church, where he painted the frescoes with Christological scenes in the second bay, from the *Nativity* to the *Road to Calvary*. In the latter scene he is flanked by a more elegant and mature artist, identified by some with Duccio, by others with Memmo di Filippuccio, Simone Martini's father-in-law.

The artist's participation in the decoration of the Upper Church took place in the last two decades of the 13th century, from the beginning when he worked alongside Cimabue in the left transept, where the execution of an angel has been attributed to him, to the collaboration with the Roman painter Torriti on the *Vault of the Saints* that covers the third bay. Later he entered the circle of Giotto's workshop and his hand has been recognized in some parts of the decoration it carried out: in the *Saint Augustine* and *Saint Ambrose* of the *Vault of the Doctors*, in the *Saint Benedict* and *Saint Clare* on the entrance archway and in the *Saint Paul* on the inside wall of the façade.

Thus his career is interesting as it constitutes a bridge between the generation of local painters steeped in the Byzantine tradition of the 13th century and the great period of the decoration of the Upper Church, cradle of Italian Gothic art.

LOWER CHURCH, SAN FRANCESCO

The nave of
the Lower Church

Master of St. Francis, *Episodes from the Life of Christ* and *Episodes from the Life of Saint Francis*, *c.* 1253

The name Master of St. Francis is used to indicate the author of a group of works realized in Assisi and bordering regions, always in Franciscan circles, who can be considered the most important Umbrian artist of the 13th century. His figurative culture is rooted in the late Byzantine repertory, reappraised on the basis of the work of Giunta Pisano, but also revivified by the encounter with the artists from beyond the Alps active in the Franciscan basilica at the start of the great decorative undertaking. Out of these influences he forged an original style, which enlivened the lineation of the figures, imbuing them with expressiveness and accents of strong characterization and revealing a complex figurative culture, rich in diverse reminiscences.

His most important works are the frescoes in the nave of the Lower Church of San Francesco, which must have been completed by 1260. Although some of them have been lost owing to the subsequent opening of the side chapels, and the characteristics of the original project, which must have envisaged a less luminous and more intimate setting, have been greatly altered, it is still possible to grasp the caliber of this first great mural cycle dedicated to St. Francis. It was here, in fact, that the official and regular representation of the saint began and that, for the first time, an iconographic parallel was established between Francis and Christ, something that would be reaffirmed several times in the decoration of the basilica. The tone of the narration is magniloquent and monumental, with a particular taste for the precious element. In fact the frescoes were intended to turn the Lower Church into a gleaming casket, in contrast with the simplicity of the original architectural scheme. For this purpose small convex mirrors were inserted in the plaster to catch the light and reflect it amidst the glitter of the gold.

Crucifixion,
detail

Deposition

Facing page,
*Lamentation
over the Body
of the Redeemer*

MULIERES SEDENTES AD MONUMEN

CENNI DI PEPO called
CIMABUE

Florence, *c.* 1240 - after 1302

"Cimabue thought to hold the field in painting, and now Giotto hath the cry, so that the other's fame is growing dim [...]" (*Purgatorio*, XI, vv. 94-6). Dante's judgment has long conditioned the attitude to Cimabue's work adopted by critics: Giotto's teacher, he was thought to have watched his rise without being able to grasp the full import of his innovative approach and was thus doomed to inevitable oblivion. We know little about him, despite the evident popularity he enjoyed in his own time, and there are few references to him in the archives: in 1272 he is documented in Rome, where he had probably gone to execute works that have now been lost. In 1301 he was in Pisa, where he undertook to complete the mosaic in the apse of the cathedral and paint a *Maestà* for the hospital of Santa Chiara, a work that has vanished or may never have been realized. His presence in Pisa is recorded again in 1302, when he received the balance of payment for the mosaic. The documents have no more to say, and so we have no choice but to proceed by conjecture, even when reconstructing the catalogue of his works. Born in Florence in the first half of the 13th century, he received his training in the city. Thus a fundamental point of reference must have been the mosaics in the baptistery of San Giovanni, whose authorship and chronology are disputed but

Andrea Bonaiuti, *Triumph of the Church Militant*, detail with portrait of Cimabue, Santa Maria Novella, Florence

which were realized under the direction of Oriental masters, perhaps from Venice. The earliest evidence for his activity as a painter is to be found in the *Crucifix* executed for the church of San Domenico in Arezzo, dating from around 1265-70: a rich and solemn work in which Cimabue reproduces the formula used by Giunta Pisano for San Domenico in Bologna, with the dead Christ and the figures of the mourners, Mary and John, set at the ends of the arms, level with Christ. A few years later the artist, back in Florence, painted the *Crucifix* for the church of Santa Croce, now in the Museo dell'Opera. The reputation he had established took Cimabue first to Pisa, where he painted a *Maestà* for the church of San Francesco that is now in the Louvre, and then to Bologna, where a panel with the same subject can still be seen in the church of Santa Maria dei Servi. But Cimabue's greatest masterpiece are the frescoes in the Upper Church of San Francesco in Assisi where, probably around 1280, he decorated the apse, the vault above the choir and part of the transept walls. Unfortunately the seepage of damp has resulted in an inversion of the shades of color, so that the pale tones have darkened and the dark tones now appear light, as in the negative of a photograph. The great *Maestà* in the Uffizi, originally in the Florentine church of Santa Trinita, dates from the same period as the frescoes in Assisi.

Left, *The Four Evangelists*, detail, Upper Church, Assisi

French Master,
Saint Paul, second
half of the 13th
century

Before Cimabue, a
painter with a foreign
training, an exponent
of the most genuine
Gothic tradition of the
Ile-de-France, had
been summoned to
work in the Upper
Church. Traces of his
work can be found in
the upper part of the
right transept and
some parts of the
apse. His presence
reflects the
Franciscans' desire to
erect a place of
worship that would be
able to rival the
Gothic cathedrals of
England and France
even in terms of
cultural modernity, as
was only fitting for
the mother house of
an order that was
taking on an
international
dimension.
This unknown but
outstanding artist was
responsible for two
"inventions" that
Cimabue and Giotto's
Tuscan group was to
translate into more
Latin forms and
disseminate in later
Italian painting: the
"diadem," i.e. the
projecting halo, which
was to prove
enormously popular
throughout the 14th
century, and the mock
architecture, the first
to be painted in fresco
in Italy.

UPPER CHURCH, SAN FRANCESCO

It is likely that Cimabue was summoned to paint in the Upper Church in order to fill the gap left by the departure, or death, of the foreign artist who had started the work in the right transept. The dating vacillates between two periods: the years 1277-80, which correspond to the papacy of Nicholas III, in the world Giovanni Gaetano Orsini and a great supporter of the Franciscan Order, and the years 1281-83, during the papacy of Martin IV, the Ghibelline pope imposed by Charles of Anjou.

In 1272 Cimabue is documented in Rome, where he was probably engaged for the work in Assisi along with a number of Roman painters, responsible for the frescoes in the upper part of the nave, above Giotto's *Legend of Saint Francis*, with scenes from the Old and New Testament. In fact the decoration of the basilica was an undertaking of a national character, carried out at the behest of the Roman Curia and under its control.

Cimabue was assigned a preeminent role in the work: he was entrusted with a highly complex cycle of frescoes, comprising scenes from the lives of Mary and the Apostles and the Apocalypse, located in a place of great prestige, the presbytery. Unfortunately the frescoes are in a very precarious state of preservation: on top of the deterioration of the white lead, which has resulted in a reversal of the relations between the light and dark shades, as in a photographic negative, and irreversible altered the chromatic value of the work, has come, in more recent times, the havoc wreaked by the earthquake of 1997, which did most damage to this part of the church, bringing down a frescoed vaulting cell.

San Francesco, Assisi. View of the
transept with the frescoes of Cimabue
and the French Master

THE APSE: *Scenes from the Life of Mary, c.* 1280

The Virgin Taking Leave of the Apostles

The first scenes, those of Mary's childhood, painted in the lunettes, have deteriorated badly and been repainted, so that they are practically impossible to decipher. On the walls are set the episodes relating to the death of the Virgin, her assumption into heaven and her triumph at Christ's side. The source of the iconography can be identified as Jacobus de Voragine's *Legenda Aurea*, a very popular text in the second half of the 13th century. Cimabue gives the various scenes an architectural setting, an expedient later adopted by Giotto as well. This is particularly evident in the scene depicting the *Virgin Taking Leave of the Apostles*, in which the halo of the only apostle standing, John, extends into the imaginary space between the two transverse arches, so that it is covered by the one in front but not the one behind. Three lamps hang from the painted vault, reinforcing the illusion of depth.

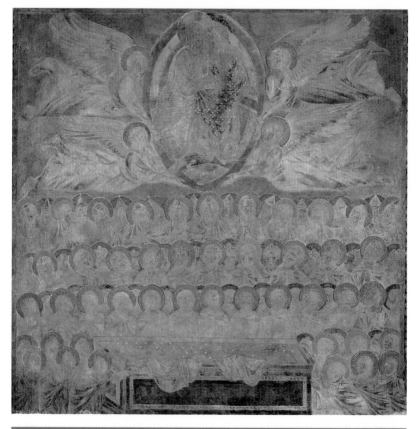

Dormitio Virginis

In the following scene, the *Dormitio Virginis* or *Death of the Virgin*, in a much worse state, the architecture is the same but the construction of the space much less accurate, owing to the passage from an earthly dimension to an other-worldly one, with the jumble of angels, patriarchs and the elect who, along with Christ, welcome the *animula* of Mary (represented as a baby in swaddling clothes).

Assumption of the Virgin

The composition is made up of three horizontal bands: at the bottom, the open sepulcher – a symbol of victory over death – with the apostles; in the middle, the patriarchs, martyrs and confessors; above, the mandorla in which Christ and the Virgin embrace. The mandorla is supported by angels, which are reminiscent of the winged victories of Roman bas-reliefs.

Christ and the Virgin in Glory

At the base of the throne, on the left, we see the Franciscan community at prayer, for whom the Virgin is interceding with Jesus Christ.

VAULT OF THE CROSSING

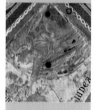

Two details of the vaulting cell of St. Matthew, completely destroyed in the earthquake of September 1997

The Four Evangelists, c. 1280

The various themes depicted in the arms of the transept, the apse and the nave are connected and linked together conceptually through the Gospels, represented by the *Four Evangelists* on the cross vault, one in each cell. Each of them, accompanied by his symbol, is inspired by an angel descending from the center of the vault, and has in front of him the city where, according to tradition, he wrote his Gospel: Corinth for Luke, Rome for Mark, Ephesus for John, Jerusalem for Matthew. It was Matthew's cell that collapsed during the 1997 earthquake.

The Evangelists, set edgeways to accentuate the sense of spatial depth, have well-characterized faces and attitudes. Matthew is reading in a reflective pose, Mark – holding a pencil – is about to start writing, while Luke is already writing and John is leafing through the pages of his Gospel. All are seated on high-backed chairs, reminiscent of the tradition of Carolingian miniatures, in front of book rests on which the writing implements are clearly identifiable. An open cabinet in the desk creates the illusion of a real space, like a genuine *trompe-l'oeil*.

Facing page:
Saint John
Saint Luke
Saint Mark
Saint Matthew

Italy or View of Rome

The representation of
"Ytalia" presents an
extraordinary
compendium of the city
of Rome in which
several monuments are
clearly recognizable:

the crenelated Castel
Sant'Angelo in the
foreground, the "Meta
Romuli" directly behind
it, St. Peter's Basilica
with its soaring
campanile, alongside the
Senatorial Palace with
the coats of arms of the

Orsini, at the back the
Capitoline Tower, the
round Pantheon, the
Militia Tower on the
left and finally, at
bottom left in the
foreground, a basilica,
perhaps that of the
Santi Apostoli.

Facing page,
Saint Matthew, detail
with _Judea_

LEFT TRANSEPT

Crucifixion, c. 1280

The great *Crucifixion*, one of the best known of all Cimabue's works in spite of its poor state of preservation, is characterized by the intense sense of drama expressed by the arched body of Christ, the exaggerated gestures of the crowd of onlookers, the tormented faces of the mourners and the frantic swirl of angels around the Cross. These elements show the extent to which Cimabue had gone beyond the tradition of Byzantine painting from which he had started out, renewing it through the vigorous accentuation of expressions and the utilization of plastic and spatial elements that we now recognize as typically Western.

At the foot of the Cross kneels St. Francis of Assisi, sharing in the suffering of Christ through the gift of the stigmata. Here too, as in the whole of the basilica's decoration, the parallel between Christ and Francis is underlined.

Cimabue and the Theme of the Crucifix

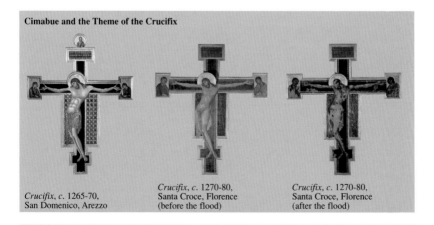

Crucifix, c. 1265-70,
San Domenico, Arezzo

Crucifix, c. 1270-80,
Santa Croce, Florence
(before the flood)

Crucifix, c. 1270-80,
Santa Croce, Florence
(after the flood)

Five Scenes of the Apocalypse, *c.* 1280

I n his representation of the scenes from Revelation, Cimabue departs significantly from the medieval iconographic tradition: spurning a detailed description of death and destruction, he dwells instead on more abstract and symbolic aspects. The presence of the *Apocalypse* in the decoration of the apse has been interpreted in different ways, depending on the date assigned to Cimabue's intervention. Those who favor the 1280s relate it to the victory of the Spiritual current at the Franciscan Chapter General of 1279, and interpret it as an allusion to the defeat of the secularizing forces of the Church led by Nicholas III Orsini. Those, on the other hand, who believe that Cimabue did his work during Orsini's papacy (1277-80) see in it a programmatic alignment with papal orthodoxy, with the clear intention of eliminating such far-fetched hypotheses as the one suggested by Bonaventura da Bagnoregio, who regarded Francis as the angel of the sixth seal and had given rise to heretical interpretations that had become widespread in Franciscan circles as well.

Vision of the Throne and the Book of the Seven Seals

*Vision of the
Angels at the Four
Corners of the
Earth*, detail

Apocalyptic Christ

Fall of Babylon,
detail

*Saint John
and the Angel*

Right Transept

Scenes from the Lives of Saints Peter and Paul, c. 1280

Saint Peter Healing the Cripple

Saint Peter Healing the Sick and Driving Out Devils

The Fall of Simon Magus

*Crucifixion
of Saint Peter*

*Decapitation
of Saint Paul*

Crucifixion

The decision to represent episodes from the lives of St. Peter and St. Paul sprang from a desire to celebrate the role
of the papacy and the Church through the example of the two
founding apostles.

In this section Cimabue's intervention seems to have been less
direct. The master was certainly responsible for the conception
of the scenes, like the one in which St. Peter heals the cripple,
where the sure construction of the architectural views constitutes one of Cimabue's fundamental contributions to Italian
painting.

Crucifixion, c. 1280

It is uncertain how much Cimabue painted of this fresco, which
is in any case in a very poor state, with the lower part almost totally missing. The composition shows evident parallels with the
other, more famous *Crucifixion*, on the wall of the left transept.

LOWER CHURCH

RIGHT TRANSEPT

Madonna and Child with Angels and Saint Francis, c. 1280

The only surviving fragment of the original decoration of the transept, much altered by repainting which makes it impossible to date the work, the fresco attests to the length of Cimabue's activity in the basilica of Assisi. It depicts the usual theme of the Madonna seated on a throne and surrounded by angels. The figure of Francis has been added on the right, isolated from the group, and may have been balanced, on the opposite side, by another saint who has now vanished. Francis is represented frontally, with the marks of the stigmata clearly visible. The type of the Virgin, in an intimate attitude and attentive to the Child, is also consonant with Franciscan spirituality, which places an emphasis on feelings of affection for the Infant Jesus and recommends poverty and humility. The wooden throne she is sitting on is not monumental in size, and is set on the same expanse of grass on which Francis is standing, barefooted.

MUSEO DELLA BASILICA DI SANTA MARIA DEGLI ANGELI

Saint Francis

The museum annexed to the basilica of Santa Maria degli Angeli houses this painting on panel, traditionally attributed to Cimabue, but probably a late copy of the portrait of Francis in the transept of the Lower Church.

Cimabue's *Maestà*

The *Madonna in Majesty* was a very common iconographic theme in the 13th and 14th centuries. Its representation was encouraged by the monastic orders and religious confraternities that regarded the Virgin as an intermediary and loving intercessor with God.
Even in a traditional theme like this, Cimabue goes beyond the formulas of Byzantine art by introducing a new and profound humanization of the figures – evident above all in the affectionate and concerned expression of Mary – and by a new sense of space, achieved by inserting the Virgin into the massive architectural structure of the throne.

Top: *Madonna Enthroned*, last quarter of the 13th century, Santa Maria dei Servi, Bologna
Maestà, last quarter of the 13th century, Uffizi, Florence
Bottom: *Maestà*, last quarter of the 13th century, Louvre, Paris
Maestà with Saints Francis and Dominic, last quarter of the 13th century, Uffizi, Florence

GIOTTO DI BONDONE

Vespignano, Vicchio di Mugello, *c.* 1267 - Florence 1337

Mentioned by Dante in the *Divine Comedy* and by Boccaccio in the *Decameron*, Giotto enjoyed a very high reputation among his contemporaries, who recognized at once the "modernity" and "naturalness" of his work. Born in the vicinity of Vicchio di Mugello in 1267, he learned the art of painting in Florence, probably in Cimabue's workshop, according to Ghiberti and Vasari. One of his earliest works is the *Crucifix* of Santa Maria Novella in Florence, dating from around 1290, which profoundly renewed the typology of the painted cross. The *Scenes from the Life of Saint Francis* frescoed in the nave of the Upper Church at Assisi are considered the finest achievement of his early career, while only part of the critics recognize Giotto's hand in the *Scenes from the Old and New Testament* above them, in the third and fourth bay. In 1300 Pope Boniface VIII called him to Rome to paint in San Giovanni in Laterano. The artist returned to the Holy City several times, among other things executing a mosaic in the basilica of St. Peter in the Vatican, of which two fragments survive. After a stay in Florence, where he painted the *Badia Polyptych* (Galleria degli Uffizi, Florence) and the *Madonna Enthroned* for the church of San Giorgio alla Costa (Museo Diocesano di Santo Stefano al Ponte, Florence), Giotto went to Rimini, where he left a beautiful *Crucifix* in the church of San Francesco. The artist then moved to Padua, where between 1303 and

Andrea Bonaiuti, *Triumph of the Church Militant*, detail with portrait of Giotto. Santa Maria Novella, Florence

1305 he painted the frescoes of the Scrovegni Chapel, considered his masterpiece and one of the cardinal works of European Gothic painting. Here the research into plastic and spatial values commenced at Assisi was taken further and, together with a softer modeling and a more harmonious coloring, gave the painting the capacity, never previously achieved, of describing all the nuances of emotion. In 1311, in Florence, he painted the *Maestà* for the church of Ognissanti, now in the Uffizi. Over the course of the second decade he went back to Assisi where, in the Lower Church, he worked on the frescoes in the chapel of the Maddalena and the transept, much of which were executed by his assistants. Giotto alternated this work with returns to Florence, where he frescoed the Peruzzi and Bardi Chapels in Santa Croce. From 1328 to 1333 he worked in Naples, for King Robert of Anjou, painting frescoes that have been lost. The signed *Polyptych* in the Pinacoteca di Bologna (only partly his own work) and the *Baroncelli Polyptych* in Santa Croce in Florence, much of it executed by Taddeo Gaddi, date from shortly afterward. In 1334, as master builder of Florence Cathedral, Giotto commenced construction of the campanile, later continued by the sculptor Andrea Pisano. In 1335 he was in Milan, where he executed works for Azzone Visconti that have now vanished. Back in Florence, he started on the decoration of the chapel in the Palazzo del Bargello, completed by the workshop after the artist's death in 1337.

Left, *The Dream of Innocent III*, detail. Upper Church, Assisi

UPPER CHURCH, SAN FRANCESCO

WALLS OF THE NAVE: UPPER PART

Frescoes of the third
bay on the right

In 1279 the Franciscan Chapter General was dominated by the current of the Spirituals, who recommended a new poverty in decoration. The immediate consequence was to be a pause in the realization of the frescoes, with the disappearance of the Roman artists who were decorating the upper part of the nave with *Scenes from the Old and New Testament*.

On the resumption of the work, with the completion of the third bay and the execution of the fourth, a new artist appeared who has been identified by some critics as the young Giotto.

The Scenes from the Life of Isaac, last quarter of the 13th century

A series of technical and compositional innovations are evident in these two scenes that suggest they are the work of a great painter, according to some a Master of Isaac, known on-

ly from these frescoes. For the majority, however, they are one of the first great achievements of the youthful Giotto, painted shortly after an apprenticeship in Rome. In fact the artist displays an ability, also recognizable in Giotto's work, to renew painting through an attentive scrutiny of reality, represented in spatial and concrete terms. In fact the artist, whoever he was, was also responsible for one of the most important innovations in the fresco technique, the laying on of the plaster in *giornate* or "days." This was a method in which the artist plastered only the part he knew he would be able to paint in a single day, and therefore only worked on fresh plaster. This allowed the paint to penetrate more deeply, greatly improving the quality and resistance of the color. Up until the arrival of this master, painters had worked at Assisi with the usual technique known as *a pontate*, i.e. by laying on portions of plaster as large as was permitted by the length of the scaffolding, with the result that they often worked on dry plaster, with large sections that were painted *a secco* and therefore much less durable. The difference between the two techniques is evident today, centuries later, in the much better state of preservation of the frescoes painted by Giotto and his workshop than those of their predecessors, such as Cimabue.

Jacob Receiving the Birthright

Isaac Rejecting Esau

Jacob Receiving the Birthright, detail

Following pages: *Isaac Rejecting Esau*, detail

This part collapsed during the earth tremor of September 26, 1997. Recently the vaulting cell with *Saint Jerome* has been put back in its original position, after over 80,000 surviving fragments of fresco had been patiently reassembled.

Scenes from the Old and New Testament and Vault of the *Doctors of the Church*, last quarter of the 13th century

The frescoes of this zone are not always on a par with the *Scenes of Isaac* and so it has been suggested that a greater part was played by the assistants who were also to work alongside Giotto in the *Scenes from the Life of Saint Francis* underneath. In addition, the 1997 earthquake caused serious damage to the vault, bringing down the vaulting cell with *Saint Jerome* and the saints set

Top: *Pentecost* and *Ascension.* Opposite, *Saint Paul* and *Saint Pieter;* bottom, *Resurrection,* detail

Vault of the *Doctors of the Church*

in aedicules. It is in the cells with the *Doctors* that the attention to contemporary reality, one of the main characteristics of Giotto's painting, is most obvious, with the exquisite representation of the polychrome effects of the Cosmatesque decorations, typical of the principal basilicas of Central and Southern Italy in those years.

WALLS OF THE NAVE, LOWER PART

Scenes from the Life of Saint Francis, late 13th century

Few doubts now remain about Giotto's authorship of the *Scenes from the Life of Saint Francis*, given the close parallels between this cycle and the Scrovegni Chapel in Padua, or the panel with the *Stigmata of Saint Francis* in the Louvre, both unquestionably his own work.

The scenes are based on St. Bonaventure of Bagnoregio's *Legenda major*, the official biography of Francis that superseded all the previous ones. According to Vasari the cycle was commissioned by Fra Giovanni da Murro, general of the order from 1296 to 1305, and we know that in 1300 Giotto was in Rome for the Jubilee proclaimed by Boniface VIII, a date that fixes a *terminus ante quem* for the realization of the greater part of the work. Analysis of the frescoes, painted using the *a giornate* system, shows that there was a total of 272 days of work, which suggests an overall duration of two or three years. The chronological order of execution of the twenty-eight scenes follows the narrative sequence of the saint's life, with the exception of the first episode.

Giotto made use of a large group of assistants, whose contribution is more evident in the last scenes, perhaps because the master had been called back to Rome. This gives us an idea of how a workshop was organized in the 14th century, with a master who designed the scenes and then, for the execution of the less prominent parts, drew on the services of a group of collaborators whose responsibilities varied according to their abilities.

The Homage of a Simple Man and The Gift of the Mantle, late 13th century

The scene depicting the homage paid to Francis by a simple man, the first scene in the order of the narration, was actually the last to be painted, owing to the presence of a transverse wooden beam, belonging to the rood screen, that got in the way of the scaffolding and whose stump is clearly visible. However, the scene cannot have been painted after 1305, as the Torre del

The Homage of a Simple Man
The Gift of the Mantle

The Admonition of the Crucifix of San Damiano

The Dream of Innocent III

Popolo in Assisi, which was finished that year, is depicted incomplete. From the stylistic viewpoint the difference between this scene and the next one, the *Gift of the Mantle*, which was executed first, is obvious: in the scene of the *Homage of a Simple Man* the painting is softer and mellower, with a velvety drapery that foreshadows the frescoes in Padua, whereas the scene of the offering of the mantle is more metallic and sharper in its tones and closer to the work of Cimabue. Some critics recognize, in the scene of the *Homage of a Simple Man*, the intervention of the so-called Master of Santa Cecilia, one of Giotto's collaborators.

The Renunciation of Possessions, late 13th century

In scenes like this the extraordinary import of Giotto's innovations is evident. They are also recognizable in the rediscovery of the eloquent gesture and in the capacity to convey feelings and states of mind, clearly exemplified by the figure of the saint's father, with his face contorted, his clothes lifted in the impulse to unleash his rage against his son, his arm held back, his fist clenched.

Giotto and the "Discovery" of Space

With Giotto the conception of space took on an organic and unitary character and the "true" story of Francis was set in an architectural space that is convincing and measurable, inhabitable and often easily recognizable, as in the depiction of San Giovanni in Laterano, where the basilica is shown in the guise it had assumed after the restoration carried out by Pope Nicholas IV in 1290.

The Dream of Innocent III

The Confirmation of the Rule

*The Vision
of the Chariot
of Fire*

*The Vision
of the Thrones*

Top: *The Expulsion of the Devils from Arezzo* and *The Ordeal by Fire before the Sultan*

Bottom, *The Ecstasy of Saint Francis* and *The Crib at Greccio*

Facing page: *The Expulsion of the Devils from Arezzo*, detail

Left: *The Crib at Greccio*, detail
Arnolfo di Cambio, *Ciborium*, 1293, Santa Cecilia in Trastevere, Rome

The Miracle of the Spring, detail
Arnolfo di Cambio, *Woman Quenching Her Thirst*, 1278-81, fragment of the Fonte Minore, 1278-81, Galleria Nazionale dell'Umbria, Perugia

Giotto and Arnolfo di Cambio

In the *Legend of Francis* at Assisi Giotto's enthusiastic embrace of the new style introduced into Central Italy by Arnolfo di Cambio is clearly apparent. In the scene of the *Crib at Greccio*, which is set with great compositional daring behind the rood screen of a church in the Romanesque style, with its Cosmatesque decorations, the ciborium is plainly inspired by Arnolfo's most recent works in Rome. At the same time the figure of the man drinking from the spring in the scene of the miracle has the classically solid corporeality of Arnolfo's figures for the fountain in Perugia.

Madonna and Child, late 13th century

Executed at the same time as the *Scenes from the Life of Saint Francis*, this beautiful picture conveys all the tenderness of the relationship between Mother and Child, who is shown smiling for the first time in Italian art.

The Miracle of the Spring

The Preaching to the Birds

Saint Francis Preaching before Honorius III, late 13th century

Here we see the first Gothic vaults to have been represented in perspective in Italian painting.

**Saint Francis
Receiving
the Stigmata**,
late 13th century

It is interesting to
compare the fresco in
Assisi and one of
Giotto's few signed
works, now in the
Louvre.

*The Death of the
Knight of Celano*

*Appearance
at the Chapter in Arles*

*The Death
of Saint Francis*

*The Vision
of Augustine
and the Bishop*

*The Verification
of the Stigmata*

Crucifix, Santa Maria
Novella, Florence

*San Giorgio
alla Costa Madonna
and Child*,
Museo Diocesano
di Santo Stefano
al Ponte, Florence

**Giotto's
"Modernity"**

The principal novelty
of Giotto's work,
already recognized in
his own time, lies in
the "modernity" of his
representation of the
real and the
contemporary, which
here is unable to avoid
a sort of self-citation.
Setting the scene inside
a church, Giotto
presents a bold view of
three works hung on
the beam of the rood
screen: at least two of
them, the *Madonna*
and the *Cross*, are
exact reproductions of
paintings by Giotto that
have come down to us.

The Last Episodes of the Legend of Saint Francis

In the last scenes the contribution of Giotto, recalled to Rome
by Boniface VIII, is less direct. Among his collaborators,
who in any case worked to his directions, it is possible to dis-
tinguish the hand of the so-called Master of Santa Cecilia,
clearly dominant in the last four scenes.

Top:

*The Lamentation of the
Poor Clares*, detail

The Canonization

*Appearance
to Gregory IX*

Facing page:

*The Healing of the
Man from Ilerda*

*The Confession of
the Woman Raised
from the Dead*

Page 70:

*The Liberation
of the Heretic Pietro*

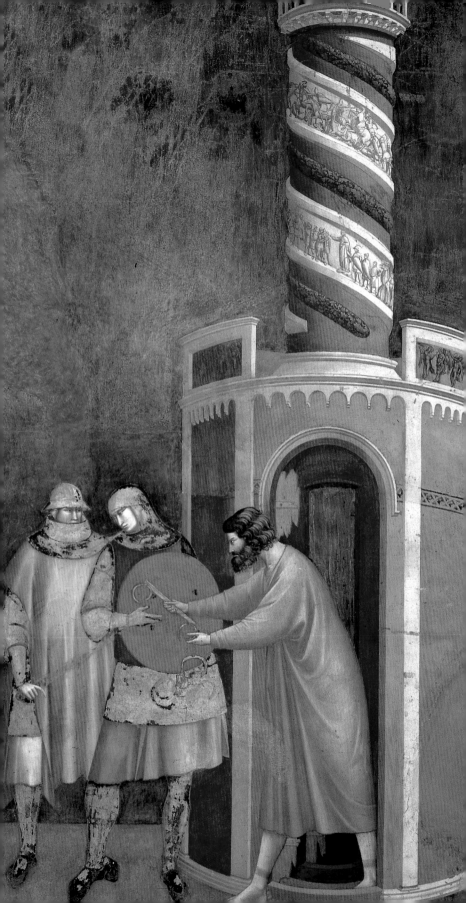

LOWER CHURCH, SAN FRANCESCO

RIGHT TRANSEPT

Scenes from the Childhood and Passion of Christ and *Miracles of Saint Francis*, early 14th century

At the beginning of the 14th century a new phase in the decoration of the Lower Church commenced, with the opening of new chapels along the nave, which entailed the destruction of part of the frescoes by the Master of St. Francis. At the same time work started on the redecoration of the right transept, which cancelled out the 13th-century intervention of Cimabue, leaving only the fresco depicting the *Madonna Enthroned with Saint Francis*. This intervention in the right transept can be attributed to some highly gifted pupils under the guidance and responsibility of Giotto himself, back in Assisi after his stay in Padua, in the first or second decade of the 14th century. Outstanding among these artists is the author of the *Scenes from the Childhood of Christ*, the *Crucifixion* and perhaps the vaulting cells of the presbytery. He was in all probability a Florentine, who also collaborated with Giotto in the chapel of the Maddalena. He is traditionally known as Giotto's Relative and can perhaps be identified with Stefano of Florence, whom Vasari said to be gifted with an "even and very agreeable" style of painting.

Visitation
Flight into Egypt
Nativity
Presentation
in the Temple
Return to Nazareth

On pages 74-5:
Slaughter
of the Innocents

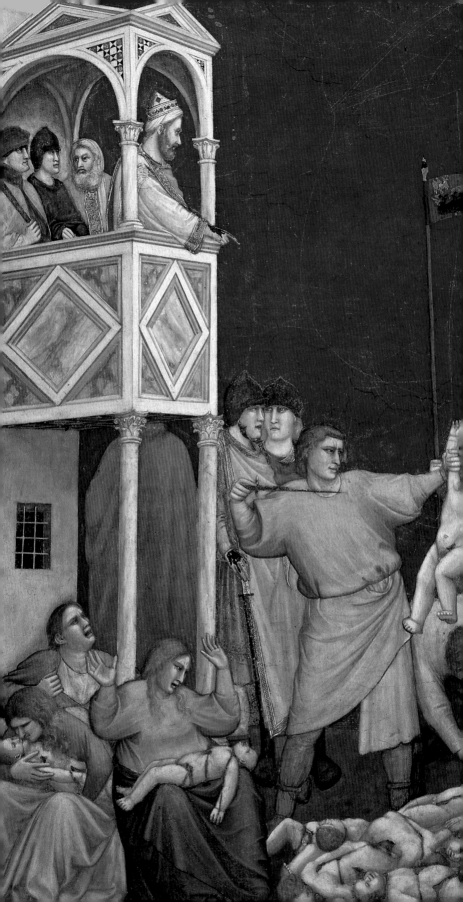

*Christ Among the
Doctors of the Church*

Crucifixion

*Saint Francis Raising
the Child Dug Out
of the Rubble*

*Saint Francis Saving
a Falling Child*

VAULTING CELLS OF THE PRESBYTERY

Allegories of the Franciscan Virtues and Glory of Saint Francis, early 14th century

The vaulting cells of the presbytery were painted on a gold ground, a highly unusual technique in a fresco owing to its

Master of St. Nicholas
or Palmerino
di Guido, *Saint
Nicholas Throwing
Three Gold Bars to
Three Poor Maidens*

*Saint Nicholas
Pardoning the Consul*

Chapel of San Nicola,
early 14th century

The chapel of San
Nicola, commissioned
by the powerful Orsini
family, was frescoed
by a slavish follower
of Giotto's style, a
faithful collaborator of
the master who was
also present in Padua
and has been given the
name of the Master of
St. Nicholas, although
he is identified by
others as Palmerino di
Guido.

difficulty and costs. Obviously we are dealing here with a climate of revision of the poverty professed by the founder of the Franciscan Order: in fact this is the point where the decoration of the basilica reaches its most sumptuous. The theme is that of the glorification of St. Francis through the construction of complex allegories extolling the principal Franciscan virtues: Poverty, Obedience and Chastity.

Angel with Stigmata

Mary Magdalene and the Donor Cardinal Pietro di Barro

Chapel of the Maddalena, early 14th century

The chapel dedicated to the Magdalen was built by the French cardinal Pietro di Barro, represented at the saint's feet, and its fresco decoration was commissioned by the bishop of Assisi, Teobaldo Pontano, represented at the feet of the patron saint of the city, Rufinus.

Almost all the critics agree that the frescoes were executed by two different artists: one, whose colors are even, mellow and soft, has been identified as Giotto following his decoration of the Scrovegni Chapel in Padua. The date of these frescoes has been the subject of much argument, especially since it was dis-

Noli me tangere

The faces and hands of the angels are modeled in pure gold, reflecting the desire for a sumptuous decoration as well as Giotto's willingness to experiment with new techniques.
Another trick, to be found in all the frescoes by the school of Giotto in the Lower Church, consists in the way the haloes are represented. Their surfaces are never set parallel to the wall, but inclined so as to pick up light from the source that was present at the time of their realization.

covered that Pontano became bishop of Assisi in 1298, and not 1314 as had previously been thought. This backdating has made it possible to ascribe the *Scenes from the Life of the Magdalen* to a period closer to the Paduan frescoes, with which they display undeniable similarities.

*Ascension
of Mary Magdalene*

*The Hermit Zosimus
Gives a Cloak to
the Magdalen*

*Voyage
of the Magdalen
to Marseilles*

SIMONE MARTINI

Siena *c.* 1284 - Avignon 1344

The earliest reference to Simone Martini is in 1315, the year in which he received loans from the Commune of Siena and signed the great fresco of the *Maestà* in the city's Palazzo Pubblico. The prestige of this work shows that the artist already enjoyed a high reputation. According to art historians, it was around this time that he moved frequently between Siena and Assisi, where he decorated the chapel of San Martino. This commission brought him into contact with the Angevin court, for which in 1317 he painted a panel depicting *Saint Louis of Toulouse*, now in the Museo di Capodimonte. A document from the same year records the award of 50 ounces of gold to Simone by Robert of Anjou, who in the meantime had made him a knight.

Returning to Tuscany, in 1319 the artist painted a large polyptych for the church of San Domenico in Pisa, now in the Museo di San Matteo, developing a complex and magnificent model of altarpiece that he replicated at Orvieto in 1320. At Siena, in 1324, Simone married Giovanna, daughter of the painter Memmo di Filippuccio and sister of Lippo Memmi, with whom he ran a large workshop. In 1333 the two artists signed the triptych with the *Annunciation* for Siena Cathedral, now in the Uffizi. Their workshop produced both altarpieces and objects of lesser value, such as standards and trappings for altars, which have unfortunately been lost. In 1330 Simone frescoed some rooms in the Palazzo Pub-

Simone Martini, presumed self-portrait, detail of the *Miracle of the Child Raised from the Dead*, Lower Church, Assisi

blico for the Commune of Siena: the large fresco of *Guidoriccio da Fogliano* has survived, although serious doubts have been raised about its date and authorship. In 1336 the painter was called to the papal court in Avignon. Here he made friends with Petrarch, decorating for him a codex that is now in the Biblioteca Ambrosiana in Milan, and painting a portrait of his beloved Laura, now lost. Only a few fragments of the works he carried out for the pope have survived, and can now be seen in the museum of the Palais des Papes. He died at Avignon in 1344.

Described by Ghiberti as a "most noble and famous painter," Simone Martini studied the work of Duccio, from whom he derived the grace of his figures and compositions. On the other hand, he also showed an interest in French Gothic art, with which he was already familiar, even before going to Avignon, through gold and ivory work and embroidery imported into Italy. In fact his painting is characterized by a great elegance and preciosity that stems not only from his style but also from the use of such materials as gold, silver and tin leaf, colored glass and enamel, in keeping with the refinement for which Sienese goldsmithry was celebrated. At the same time Simone was an acute observer of the world around him, conferring great expressiveness and lively gestures on his figures and carefully depicting their features: Simone was responsible for the first individual portraits in medieval painting.

Left, Simone Martini, *Knighting of Saint Martin*, Lower Church, Assisi

LOWER CHURCH, SAN FRANCESCO

CHAPEL OF SAN MARTINO, 1312-1317

The chapel was built in 1312 by Brother Gentile Partino da Montefiore, who had been made a cardinal in 1298 by Boniface VIII with the title of Martino ai Monti (the reason why the chapel is dedicated to St. Martin). His coat of arms is repeated several times in the splays of the windows and he himself is portrayed in fresco, on the inside of the front wall, holding out his hand to St Martin, and in the stained glass of the central two-light window. In 1307 the cardinal had been sent to Buda as papal legate to place Robert of Anjou's nephew Carobert on the throne of Hungary, and had brought back lavish gifts for the basilica. For some time the Angevins had had important

Facing page:
*Saint Martin
and the Donor*, detail

links with the Franciscan Order, and with the current of the Spirituals in particular, at least since Louis had renounced his throne to become a friar, taking a vow of absolute poverty. The dating of the frescoes oscillates between 1312, the year in which the documents tell us that Gentile da Montefiore was in Assisi and Siena (and thus came into contact with Simone Martini), and 1317, the year of the canonization of Louis of Anjou, bishop of Toulouse, portrayed on the underside of the entrance arch (traditionally the last part to be frescoed). This chronology is corroborated by the women's clothing, which is in the style that was in fashion in the first two decades of the 14th century.

Saint Martin and the Division of the Cloak

Born in Pannonia in the 4th century, Martin, the son of a tribune in the Roman army, renounced arms in the year 344 to devote himself to religion. He was a saint rarely represented in Italy, and Simone probably lacked precise iconographic references. In fact he chose to tell his story in eight episodes, four of them relating to his secular and worldly life, before giving himself up totally to a religious one, and four to the last part, completely ignoring the central period in Martin's existence (his discipleship under St. Hilary of Poitiers and the time he spent as a hermit and in a monastery), even though this must have been of great importance.

In the first four scenes Martin is depicted as an elegant man of the world, in a profane and stately setting that recalls the atmosphere of the courts of the 14th century. This scene represents the most famous episode, the one in which he shares his cloak with a beggar.

Martin's Dream

Jesus Christ appears to Martin in a dream, wrapped in the cloak he had given to the beggar and accompanied by a host of angels. In this indoor scene two elements characteristic of Simone's painting are present: his skillful construction of space, evident in the overlapping of the angels' haloes, and the attention paid to elements of reality: the bed in which Martin is lying is draped with a fine coverlet of Sienese cloth and a sheet decorated with openwork embroidery.

Note how the checked pattern of the bedcover is distorted to follow the shape of the saint's body.

Knighting of Saint Martin

"The whole of the Middle Ages is in it," said Théophile Gautier of this fresco. And in effect with this episode, which is not recorded in the saint's biography, it appears that Simone wanted to conjure up his own knighting by Robert of Anjou, the king of Naples whose dynasty is celebrated in the chapel. In fact, the Roman soldier Martin is transformed into a medieval *miles*, with particular attention paid to the courtly and aristocratic surroundings, characterized by the presence of musicians, singers and squires with arms and a falcon. This responds not only to Simone's undeniable penchant for refined and chivalrous circles, but also to the expectations of his aristocratic clients.

Martin Renouncing Arms

The figure of the emperor Julian, practically identical to the one in the previous scene, recalls the profile portraits on ancient Roman coins, which probably served as a model, while the figure of Martin stands out in the middle, at the intersection of the diagonals formed by the profiles of the figures in the two enemy camps. Here too Simone does not neglect to depict the elegant attire of the young knight and the people that surround him. Note the use of gold leaf in the decorations of the clothing and furnishings, in the coins and in the saint's splendid halo.

Saint Martin
in Meditation

Saint Martin in Meditation
and *Saint Martin and the Miraculous Mass*

From the fifth scene onward the episodes relate to the last period of Martin's life, when he was bishop of Tours. In the first the saint, absorbed in a profound ecstasy, is called by two acolytes to celebrate Mass in the chapel represented in perspective in the background. The figure of Martin, rapt in meditation and gleaming with gold, makes a beautiful contrast with the concerned and attentive gesture of the young deacon, with stubble sprouting on his face, who is attempting to arouse him.

In the second, Martin, after giving his tunic to a leper, celebrates Mass: as he raises the Host two angels bring him a length of precious cloth. Once again the realistic representation of the details is evident in the depiction of the altar, covered by two typical "Umbrian altar cloths," and in the timid gesture of the deacon who watches the apparition in amazement. The episode, here depicted for the first time in Italy, took place at Albenga.

Saint Martin and
the Miraculous Mass

Saint Martin and the Miracle of the Boy Raised from the Dead

Unfortunately the fresco is fairly badly damaged, especially in the central part, where the miraculous resurrection takes place. The varied and animated group of praying onlookers is more legible. Among them stands out the man on the right, dressed in blue, who observes the scene with a skeptical air and is rebuked by his companion dressed in green: it is probably a self-portrait. The building behind has been identified as the Palazzo Pubblico of Siena prior to the construction of the Torre del Mangia. According to the official hagiographies, the miracle had occurred in the countryside of Chartres, but Simone has chosen to transfer it, with a touch of civic pride, to the city of Siena, where the legend of a great miracle worked by St. Martin when he passed through on his way to Rome was current.

Behind the child's mother we see an old woman dressed as a penitent. This has traditionally been seen as a homage to St. Clare of Montefalco, an Umbrian mystic who had died in 1308 and was held in much esteem in the ecclesiastic circles of the time.

Saint Martin and the Miracle of the Fire

Emperor Valentinian is kneeling at the saint's feet since, after refusing to receive him, he has been hurled to the ground by a tongue of flame springing suddenly from the throne.
Scenes like this clearly reveal Simone's debt to the spatial inventions of Giotto, showing how confidently the Sienese painter is able to handle them.

Death of Saint Martin, detail

Funeral of Saint Martin, detail

Saint Louis of Toulouse Crowning Robert of Anjou King of Naples, 1317, detail

Death and **Funeral of Saint Martin**

The two scenes are similar in their spatial construction and composition. They even contain the same figures. In particular one of the two knights under the aedicule in the death scene reappears wearing a hood in the scene of the funeral, and bears a remarkable resemblance to Robert of Anjou, portrayed by Simone in the *Saint Louis Altarpiece*, in the Museo di Capodimonte, Naples.

*Death of
Saint Martin*

*Funeral of
Saint Martin*

The Saints on the Underside of the Arch

T he eight saints depicted on the underside of the arch, in addition to throwing light on the date of the work, as has already been pointed out, help to determine the nature of the commission, in which there is an evident intent to glorify the House
of Anjou and its links with the Franciscan Order. Alongside
Francis, Clare and Anthony, saints connected with the order, we
find personages connected with the figure of Robert of Anjou:
Louis of Toulouse was his brother, Elizabeth of Hungary was
the aunt of his mother Mary, Louis of France was his great
grandfather and Mary Magdalene and Catherine were saints to
whom his father Charles was particularly devoted.

The figure of St. Louis
was evidently painted
at a later date, over a
figure dressed in a long
white tunic, still visible
at the bottom

Top: *Saint Louis of France
and Saint Louis of Toulouse
Saint Anthony of Padua
and Saint Francis*

Underneath: *Saint Mary Magdalene
and Saint Catherine of Alexandria
Saint Clare and Saint Elizabeth of
Hungary*

Saint Benedict

Eighteen saints are portrayed at half-length in the splays of the two-light windows. They are not all identifiable owing to the almost total disappearance of the gilt inscriptions that accompanied them.

Saint Mary Magdalene and Saint Catherine of Alexandria, detail

The Stained-Glass Windows, 1312-17

We know nothing of the craftsmen who made the stained-glass windows, but their designs can plausibly be attributed to Simone. Indeed, two considerations suggest that this was his first intervention, in order of time, in the decoration of the chapel: the stylistic affinity with the *Maestà* in the Palazzo Pubblico of Siena and the custom of realizing the windows before the decorations on the walls, so that they could be painted under conditions in which the light was already filtered through the stained glass, which alters the perception of the images.

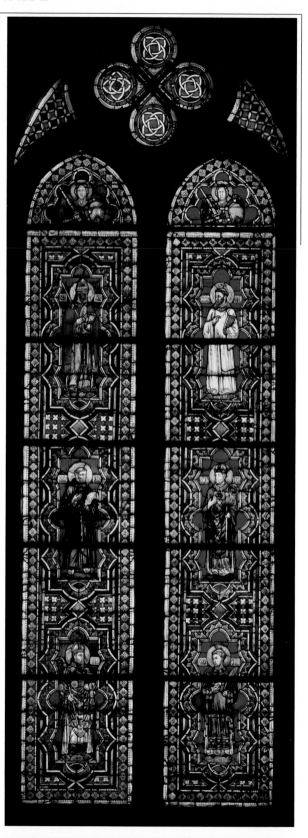

RIGHT TRANSEPT

Madonna and Child between Two Saints
and *Five Saints*, 1317-19

The frescoes, which according to Vasari were started by Simone and finished by Lippo Memmi, used to decorate an altar dedicated to St. Elizabeth of Hungary. Located in the right arm of the transept, it was commissioned by Mary, daughter of the king of Hungary, wife of Charles II of Anjou and great-niece of St. Elizabeth, mother of Louis of Toulouse and Robert of Anjou and herself a Franciscan tertiary. The personages represented are, once again, linked to the Angevin dynasty and the Fran-

ciscan Order. On the rear wall five saints are presented, apparently standing behind a marble parapet and separated by the slender columns of a loggia: St. Francis, St. Louis of Toulouse, St. Elizabeth of Hungary, St. Margaret (in the past mistakenly thought to be St. Clare) and a handsome young prince, who has fairly recently been identified as St. Henry, the son of St. Stephen, king of Hungary, who flanks the Virgin on the adjoining wall, along with St. Ladislas. The dating varies between 1317, the year of Louis's canonization, and 1323, the year of Mary of Hungary's death. A credible *terminus ante quem* seems to be 1319, as in that year the Guelphs were driven out of Assisi and the resulting tensions would have made any work on the basilica impossible.

PIETRO LORENZETTI

Siena *c.* 1280/85 - 1348?

Along with Simone Martini and his brother Ambrogio, Pietro Lorenzetti was one of the leading figures in Sienese art, whose fame spread beyond the confines of the city, earning him prestigious commissions from every part of Central Italy. However, there are few documents relating to the two brothers, and even their dates of birth and death remain uncertain. Probably born in Siena around 1280, Pietro received his training in the workshop of Duccio di Buoninsegna, from whom he derived the grace and tenderness of his images of the Madonna and Child. His figures attain a poignant intimacy in works like the polyptych in the parish church of Santa Maria in Arezzo, executed in 1320 for Bishop Guido Tarlati, or the so-called *Madonna of the Smile*, frescoed in the Lower Church at Assisi. This last work is part of a decoration carried out in the Lower Church, probably in several different phases over the first twenty years of the 14th century. Here the painter reveals that he had also assimilated the lesson of Giotto in the construction of solid figures and complex compositions, as is evident in the *Scenes of the Passion*, or the panel with the *Nativity of the Virgin* painted for Siena Cathedral. In these works, moreover, the painter shows a keen interest in everyday life, enriching his compositions with curious and engaging anecdotes. While remaining faithful to models of Byzantine derivation, in the scene of the *Deposition of Christ* in Assisi for example, he brings a new and intense dramatic force to his narration, which has a parallel in the sculpture of Giovanni Pisano, long active in Siena.

In 1324 Pietro Lorenzetti is recorded in Siena, where he was paid for the decoration of the *Libro del Capitano del Popolo*, and in 1326 for some paintings executed for the Vestry Board of Santa Maria, works that have both been lost. In 1329 he signed the large polyptych for the Carmelite Church, now in the Pinacoteca Nazionale of Siena. Between 1335 and 1342 the artist was at work on the triptych depicting the *Nativity of the Virgin* for the altar of San Savino in Siena Cathedral, a painting that can now be seen in the Museo dell'Opera del Duomo. In 1335 he executed, in collaboration with his brother Ambrogio, the decoration of the façade of the Spedale di Santa Maria della Scala, frescoed with *Scenes from the Life of the Virgin* that have not survived, but which are testified by the numerous derivations of them to be found in the work of other Sienese painters. Between 1340 and 1343 he painted the panel with the *Madonna Enthroned* for the church of San Francesco at Pistoia but now in the Uffizi in Florence. Like his brother Ambrogio, Pietro Lorenzetti probably died during the terrible outbreak of the Black Death in 1348.

Left, *Crucifixion*, detail. Lower Church, Assisi

LOWER CHURCH, SAN FRANCESCO

LEFT TRANSEPT

The frescoes painted in the left transept of the Lower Church of San Francesco can probably be considered Pietro Lorenzetti's first major work. The decoration was executed in various phases, something that is also apparent from the evolution of his style: the influence of Duccio, obvious in the oldest parts, was subsequently enlivened by a personal meditation on the work of Giotto, who may have been in the Lower Church in the same years, decorating the right transept and the chapel of the Maddalena with his workshop.

The triptych frescoed in the Orsini Chapel must date from the first phase, in 1310-15; the six scenes of the *Passion* from the second (1315-19); the *Crucifixion*, the *post mortem* scenes and *Saint Francis Receiving the Stigmata*, on the other hand, would have been painted in the years 1320-24. Here we will follow, as far as possible, the order in which the scenes were executed.

Madonna and Child between Saints John the Baptist and Francis, 1310-15

The triptych is painted in fresco on the entrance wall of the chapel of San Giovanni, founded by Cardinal Napoleone Orsini, and its composition is based on the scheme of the devotional image, with the Madonna in the middle and the two saints at the sides, looking out over a balustrade and separated by

arches, on a gold ground. Francis and the Baptist are indicating, with the same gesture of the finger pointing downward, the way to be followed by the faithful. One of the most poetic of Pietro Lorenzetti's paintings, the triptych is characterized by a great sense of tenderness, manifested above all in the intense dialogue between the Madonna and Child and the way that the four figures are linked by an exchange of glances.

Entry of Christ into Jerusalem, 1315-19

T he complex and animated scene is characterized by the brilliant colors of the buildings in the background, the variety of faces and expressions in the two processions that surround Jesus, the apostles on the left and the inhabitants of Jerusalem on the right, and the overall sense of fluid and calm movement.

Washing of the Feet, 1315-19

I n this scene Pietro overcomes, with a skillful and confident handling of the composition, the obstacle presented by a real arch, creating a scene of great precision in its definition of space, laid out on two levels.

Last Supper, 1315-19

In this superbly composed scene, our attention is caught by the view of the kitchen, on the left: a piece of masterful painting, in which the bold perspective of the fireplace and the convincing depth of the niches with utensils in them reveal the degree of intelligence with which Pietro was able to handle space. The choice of such a marginal episode, with the servants cleaning the dishes, the dog eating the leftovers and the cat drowsing, can be seen as a sign of Pietro's attention to the elements of daily life, but it has also been interpreted symbolically, with the kitchen scene viewed as an allusion to the Jewish Passover, the sacrifice of actual meat in the Old Testament, while the new festival of Easter, with the spiritual Lamb, is being celebrated in the next room.

The composition attests to the Gothic roots of the painter's figurative culture, with the unusual architectural structure and its decorative fantasies, inspired by Parisian illuminated manuscripts and examples of gold work.

Arrest of Christ, 1315-19

In the *Last Supper* the moon had just risen outside the pavilion. In the *Arrest* hours have passed and the moon is setting in the beautiful starry sky that forms a silent backdrop to the drama of the Christ's betrayal, represented by the kiss of Judah and his abandonment by the apostles, who are moving away behind him, with their faces hidden.

Flagellation before Pilate and *Road to Calvary*, 1315-19

In the *Flagellation before Pilate* the narrative continues in chronological order. In fact it is now daytime and the moon and stars have vanished. The scene is animated by a feeling of deep tension and unease, enriched by curious architectural elements of great beauty. The tension slackens in the slow progress of the procession along the *Road to Calvary*, which follows the customary circular course as it emerges from the walls of Jerusalem.

Crucifixion, 1315-19

The cross is surrounded by a varied and teeming ring of soldiers, horsemen and followers of Jesus, in which the elevation of Mount Calvary is used to open up the scene like a fan to the observer. Cimabue's screaming crowd has been replaced by a stage on which an intense exchange of glances takes place, revealing the manifold reactions of those present, realistically characterized as individuals: "here the multitude has a face," Cesare Brandi has aptly observed.

This varied and lively throng is set against the limpid splendor of the sky, in which the angels hold their mournful dance, their halos as luminous as stars.

Deposition and *Burial of Christ*, 1320-24

The two scenes are constructed according to the modern principles of composition established by Giotto: in the *Deposition* the pyramid of figures leaves dramatically free the space on the right, where the cross stands alone; in the *Burial* the mourners gather closely around the body of Christ in their distress. In both episodes there is a strong sense of drama, most evident in some of the details: the intense gaze of the Virgin at her dead son, the face of the Magdalen in the second scene, locked up in her grief, and the trickle of blood that stands out against the white of the stone, in the *Deposition*.

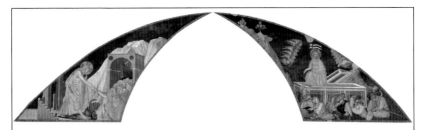

Resurrection, 1320-24

Descent into Limbo and Resurrection

In the scene of the *Resurrection* Pietro skillfully exploits the restricted space imposed on him by the triangular wall: in his asymmetrical position the Risen Christ takes on a wholly central value. At the foot of the tomb the bodies of the sleeping soldiers are represented with bold foreshortening. They depict well-characterized human types: those of a fragile and coarse humanity, contrasted with the sturdy figure of Christ victorious over death.

Descent into Limbo, 1320-24

In this scene, less innovative than the others from the viewpoint of composition, it has been suggested that Pietro played a less direct part and more responsibility was given to the workshop.

Saint Francis Receiving the Stigmata, 1320-24

With this scene the story of Christ's Passion is interrupted and a Franciscan parenthesis introduced with the clear aim of placing the suffering of Jesus and the way of salvation indicated by Francis on parallel planes. It is no co-incidence that this episode occupies the place that should have been dedicated to the *Agony in the Garden of Gethsemane*, to which clear reference is made by the presence of olive trees (the Hebrew word *gethsemani* means an oil press) and the friar who, like the apostles, is unaware of the miracle, absorbed instead in reading his prayer book.

Judas Hanged, 1320-24

The source chosen for this terrible image is the Apocryphal Gospel of Nicodemus, in which Judas hangs himself from a beam of his house, and not from the fig tree found in the most common representation. But what is most striking is the realistic way in which Judas's mutilated body is depicted, with the neck dislocated, the body drooping and the belly slit, as in the hanged men that Pietro must have seen, left on the gallows for days, as frequently happened in medieval cities. The figure of the treacherous apostle, unlike any other in the cycle, is also identified by an inscription, *[I]scariota*.

Madonna and Child with Saints Francis and John the Evangelist, 1320-24

Under the large *Crucifixion*, on the right, Pietro painted a second triptych on a gold ground that has the Madonna and Child at its center: the Infant Jesus questions his Mother who indicates Francis, on her right, with her thumb and invites Christ to bless him with her gaze. On the right St. John seems to be on the point of joining in the "Holy Conversation." There is no architectural structure separating the figures and they are intertwined in a dialogue of gestures and gazes. Below is painted a crucifix that, together with Francis's gesture, displaying the stigmata, invites the faithful to a further reflection on the mystery of sorrow and on the Franciscan example of the imitation of Christ.

Madonna and Child with Saints Francis and John the Evangelist, detail

Pietro Lorenzetti and Illusionistic Painting

On the rear wall of the transept, below St. Rufinus, St. Catherine of Alexandria, St. Clare and St. Margaret, is painted a bench set against the wall, covered with a rich drape trimmed with fur. It is a piece of bravura painting, a *trompe-l'œil* that is enriched with other details: the mock panels of marble on the wall against which the bench is set and, on the adjoining wall, right underneath the fake altar onto which face the Virgin and the Child with St. Francis and St. John the Evangelist, a niche containing a book and a small ampulla. All these elements, painted illusionistically, form a sort of mock chapel.

Bibliography

U. Gnoli, *Pittori e miniatori dell'Umbria*, Spoleto 1923

Giotto e i giotteschi in Assisi, Rome 1969

Il Tesoro della Basilica di San Francesco ad Assisi, Assisi 1980

L. Bellosi, *Giotto*, Florence 1981

L. Bellosi, *La pecora di Giotto*, Turin 1985

M. Chiellini, *Cimabue*, Florence-New York 1988

C. Frugoni, *Pietro and Ambrogio Lorenzetti*, Florence-New York 1988

C. Frugoni, *Francesco e l'invenzione delle stimmate. Una storia per parole e immagini fino a Bonaventura e Giotto*, Turin 1988

C. Jannella, *Simone Martini*, Florence-New York 1989

Dizionario della pittura e dei pittori, Turin 1989-94

C. De Benedictis, "Pietro Lorenzetti," in *Enciclopedia dell'Arte Medievale*, VII, Rome 1996

E. Lunghi, *The Basilica of St Francis in Assisi*, Florence 1996

S. Romano, "Maestro di San Francesco" in *Enciclopedia dell'Arte Medievale*, VIII, Rome 1997